THE CASTLE ON THE ISLAND OF LUNDY

This booklet is offered in celebration of the 750 years
that the castle has stood on Lundy
and of its restoration by the Landmark Trust

The castle from the north-west, 1775. (Grose, F. *Antiquities of England & Wales* 1776, Vol 4.)

THE CASTLE ON THE ISLAND OF LUNDY

750 Years
1244–1994

MYRTLE TERNSTROM

For Emily, Lizzie and Jonathan

Published in a limited edition of 1000 copies, 1994 by
Myrtle Ternstrom, Whistling Down, Sandy Lane Road,
Cheltenham GL53 9DE

ISBN 0 9523062 0 4

Produced by Alan Sutton
Publishing Ltd, Stroud, Glos.
Printed in Great Britain.

Acknowledgements

I am most grateful to the following who have given their kind permission for the use of illustrations:

British Library: Drawing of King Henry III, MS Cotton Julius E IV. Woodcut of Thomas Benson, Ref. BL 851.f.38
John Dyke: Drawings of Benson's Cave and Signal Cottages. 1954 stamp showing the castle. Map of Lundy.
The Lundy Field Society: Photograph of Coastguard Cottages, H. Jukes
Mrs C. Maddy: Photograph of Signal Cottages, 1906
The Society for the Protection of Ancient Buildings: Photograph of Cable Hut, plan of the castle, and text of the report, 1928
Caroline Thackray – Plan of the castle and environs, 1988
Christopher Wright – Photograph of the interior of Benson's Cave

I also wish to thank David and Caroline Thackray for access to *The National Trust Archaeological Survey: Lundy, Devon* Vols 1 & 2, 1989, and John Dyke for assistance with material from the Lundy Museum Archives.

Cover Illustrations

Outside front: A fanciful representation of the castle. (*Historical Descriptions . . . of the Antiquities of England & Wales, c.* 1786, Boswell, Sir Alexander.)

Outside back: 1954 1 Puffin stamp. One of a set issued to commemorate the Jubilee of the first issue of Lundy stamps. The 1954 issue was the first with multi-coloured pictorials. (Designer: John Dyke.)

Inside front: Watercolour of the castle, 1927, by Miss M.F. Heaven. (Lundy Museum Archive.)

Detail from the 1927 painting by Miss M.F. Heaven, showing the Cable Hut in use as the post office. The letterbox is attached to the telegraph pole, and the cable entry point is below the box. The notice reads 'E.R. Anyone damaging this hut will be prosecuted by command of the Postmaster General'.

Inside back: Sketch of the Signal Cottages and post office *c.* 1908 showing the Allday family, the postbox inset in the window, and some Lundy stamps with GPO and Lundy postmarks. (Drawing: John Dyke.)

The island is 3¼ miles long and about ½ at the widest part.

North Light

Subterranean Passage

Long Roost

Devils Slide

Jenny's Cove

The Battery

The Old Light

Pilot's Quay

Montagu Steps

Great Shutter R.K

Hen and Chicken's

Virgins Spring

North Light

Puffin Slope

John o'Groats House

North End

Hut Circles

Gannet's Rock

Gannet's Bay

Mousehole and Trap

Gannet's Rock

Widow's Tenement (Site of)

Brazen Ward

Three Quarter Wall

Round Tower (Site of)

Tibbetts Hill

Tibbetts Point

Knight Templar Rock

The Cheeses

Half-way Wall

Logan Stone

Devils Chimney

Pondsbury

V.C. Quarry

Quarry

Quarry Bay

Quarter Wall Cottages (in ruins)

Quarter Wall

Brick field

Old Light

Sugar Loaf

Ladies Beach

Site of Chapel

Giants Graves

Farm

St Helen's Church

Millcombe House

Hotel

Landing Beach

Marisco Castle

Rat I.

Devils Limekiln

South Light

Millcombe

St Helen's Church

The Castle 13th Century

JOHN DYKE

Shutter Rock.

The castle on Lundy is magnificently situated, rising as if it were an extension of the very granite on which it stands. It commands the landing bay, and when it was built it also commanded the only path to the plateau. In itself it is small, a fort rather than a true castle, but what it lacks in grandeur it possesses in scale, and the dignity of being appropriate both to its setting and its purpose.

The first thing to be said is that although it has been referred to as Marisco Castle for generations, it was not built by the de Mariscos, but by King Henry III. The king was beset by political troubles throughout his reign, and coastal fortifications were important as he was ever conscious of the danger of his rebellious barons making an alliance with his enemies in France, Scotland, Ireland or Wales. So the king's castle was erected on Lundy to defend his realm from the pirates and outlaws who infested the Bristol Channel, and who used the fortress nature of Lundy to suit their own purposes.

Such was the situation after 1235, when William de Marisco took possession of the island. He was a member of the branch of the de Marisco family that had property in Ireland, where his father, Geoffrey, had formerly been Justiciar for the king. Geoffrey, his sons, and his nephew had all been in trouble for their part in Earl Richard's rebellion in 1234, although their lands were soon restored to them in 1235. That same year William was suspected of being responsible for the murder of one of the king's messengers at Westminster, and he fled to Lundy for safe hiding. His presence there was an offence on two counts – firstly because he was an outlaw, and secondly because the island was not his property, but belonged to his cousin, who had the same name. Once installed on Lundy, he had to sustain his existence somehow: 'William de Marisco . . . having attached to himself many outlaws and malefactors, subsisted by a piracy of goods, more especially of wine and provisions, making frequent sudden eruptions on the adjacent lands, spoiling and injuring the realm by land and sea, and native as well as foreign merchants in various ways. . . .'[1] He stayed there until 1242, when the king went to war with France, and determined measures were taken to clear the Bristol Channel of those who were both pirates and enemies.

In May 1242 William, with his band of sixteen men, was sitting at dinner on Lundy when the king's soldiers managed to make a landing under cover of mist. Instead of raising the alarm, the man who was on

1

July 25th, 1242. William de Marisco was dragged from Westminster to the
Tower before his execution. (*The Drawings of Matthew Paris*, Ed. M.R. James,
Walpole Society, 1926.)

guard betrayed his fellow outlaws, and they were all taken prisoner.
When the captives reached London, William was brought to trial, but
the charges against him were not murder and piracy alone. In 1238 an
attempt had been made on the king's life, the culprit had named
William as instigator of the plot, and so he was on trial for the gravest
crime of all, which was treason.

William confessed to piracy, but swore that he was 'free from and
utterly guiltless of the crime of high treason charged against him and
the shame of the death of the before-mentioned clerk (messenger) and
that his only motive for withdrawing to the Island had been by
avoiding to turn aside the anger of the King, which by whatever
judicial expiation . . . it had always been his first wish to appease, but
when he had fled to the Island and called some friends to his
assistance, he was driven . . . to support his wretched existence on
necessities snatched from every quarter'.[1] Nevertheless, he was
convicted and sentenced to be hung, and 'his wretched body divided
into quarters which were sent to the four principal cities in the
kingdom, by what pitiable spectacle to strike terror into all beholders.'[1]
Whether he was the victim of political intrigue or was indeed guilty, we
can not judge.

The king was so pleased to have overcome the outlaws at last that
he gave an order for 'Walter Alardi, who brought news to the King of

the capture of William de Mariscis, to have 10 marks of the King's gift.'[2] The king did not allow the rightful William de Marisco to have Lundy back again, but took it into his own hands and made no delay in arranging for it to be fortified and guarded. Indeed, he judged Lundy's importance such that he appointed William de Cantilupe, Seneschal of the Royal Household, to oversee the installation of a garrison and the construction of a fort. In July William de Cantilupe and his party set out from Bristol for Lundy, where their first task was to repair the buildings 'so that the King's Knights and Sergeants keeping it in the winter can dwell there safely'.[2] Recent archaeological excavations have shown that the Marisco's dwelling lay in the area now called Bull's Paradise, and that it must have been a stronghold, since one of the walls was found to be seven feet thick.[3]

In 1243 the sheriff of Devon was instructed to 'take with him a man skilfull, faithfull and discreet in masons work to the island of Lundy, and by his counsel and that of the Constable there choose a suitable site for a good tower with a bailey-wall, to be fortified with good lime and stone; and to begin and continue the work by the counsel of the Constable, out of the issue of the sale of rabbits . . . till the tower is finished.'[2] 2,500 skins were taken in 1243, when rabbits were a rare and valued commodity. In 1275 the annual take of rabbits was estimated at 2,000, and the value of the skins was 5s.6d. per

King Henry III, who ordered the building of the castle in 1243. (By permission of the British Library: Cotton MS Julius EIV.)

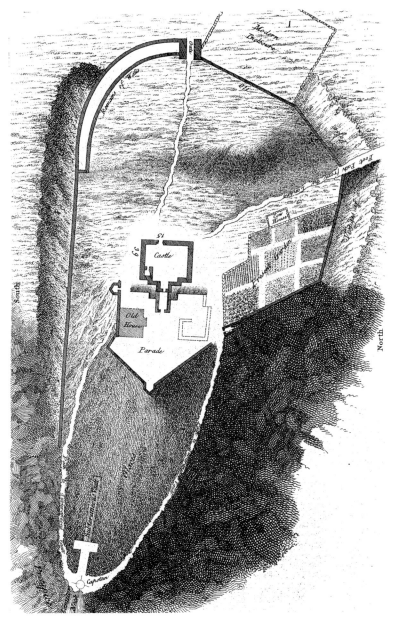

Plan of the Castle in 1776 (Grose, ibid). The dimension of the west wall should read 51.

Mauger de Sancto Albino, one of the keepers of the castle appointed by the king *c*. 1264. Memorial in Georgeham Church. (Photo: A. & M. Langham.)

100, which represented a very good income at that time, when a gallon of wine could be had for three pence.[4]

The references to Lundy in the king's documents are numerous – provisions for wages, for boats and supplies, and for the appointment of constables. The constable's force consisted of 'twenty sergeants receiving 6*d*. each daily, 20 sergeants and four mariners receiving 2½*d*. each daily, and one sergeant, Constable of the said sergeants receiving 8*d*. daily', as well as two ploughmen, two shepherds, and a dairymaid.[2] The population thus rose to more than fifty. By May of 1244 the castle was completed and, apart from the revenues from the rabbits, it had cost the king some £200.[5] The walls of the fort were nearly three feet thick, in length measured 38 by 51 feet, and there was a parade at the front (east) with bastions in the enclosing wall. On the landward side the outer defences were a curtain wall and a fosse. All being ready, 2,000 quarrels (arrows) were sent for armaments, and Richard de Clifford was appointed constable.[6, 2]

For the next 38 years a succession of different keepers was appointed, of whom this was the first: 'The king to all . . . greeting. Know ye, that we have committed our island of Lundy to the keeping of Henry de Tracy, during pleasure, together with the stock and profits of the said island.'[7] It should not be assumed that the keepers themselves took residence on the island or, indeed, that they ever went there. They were persons of substance who enjoyed the confidence of the king and who were entrusted with a grant of the island and its castle. They took what profits they could, and their responsibility was to keep Lundy guarded safely from the king's enemies. In 1254, the year of his marriage, the king's son, Edward, was given Lundy together with huge grants of land in Ireland, Wales, and Bristol. The Prince continued the appointment of keepers, and some of the changes that followed would have been accounted for by the shifting political loyalties of the times, which were turbulent. That the custody of castles was of great importance is evident, in that the dissident barons forced the king in 1258 to agree that 'Royal castles should be entrusted to Englishmen' and 'No castle on the coast or an island should be granted at farm without the agreement of the council of the whole realm'. In return, the guardians of the king's castles were to 'keep the castles of the King loyally and in good faith for the use of the King and of his heirs'.[8] When the barons defeated the king at the battle of Lewes (1264) they replaced the royal keeper with one of their own supporters, and he was just as quickly removed when Prince Edward regained control of the kingdom in the following year.[9] In 1275, his third year as king, Edward I caused a report to be made on Lundy: '. . . in summer, even in time of peace, it is necessary to have fourteen servants and a Constable to watch the defences of the island, and in winter ten servants'.[4] Following the survey and valuation, the king leased the island to Oliver de Dynan at 20 shillings a year from 1275 until 1281 when, at last, it was restored to Sir William de Marisco.[10] After his death in 1284 there followed a period of confused and disputed ownership, which reflected the troubled state of the kingdom.

The castle was one of the casualties of these troubles, for a valuation made in 1322 states that there was '. . . a certain castle with a barton (farmyard), for which they made no valuation, as the same was destroyed and burned by the Scots.'[11] In that year Lundy was held by Sir John de Wyllenton, but his lands were forfeit after he took part in the Earl of Lancaster's rebellion, and the king (Edward II) made a grant of Lundy to Hugh le Despencer the younger and his wife. Despencer was Edward's favourite and companion, but when they attempted to take refuge on the island in 1326, they were not successful. Bad weather forced them back to the South Wales coast, where they were captured by the rebel forces of the queen. Despencer was executed, the king was murdered, Lundy was once again forfeit, and was given into the care of keepers until it was returned to the de Wyllentons in 1327.

In 1333 the disputed ownership was finally resolved when William de Montacute, First Earl of Salisbury, bought the title to Lundy from the three who had claim to it: Herbert de Marisco, Ralph de Wyllenton, and Hugh le Despencer's son and heir.[12] The island then passed in succession and came into the possession of the Grenvile family. During their ownership it was a sanctuary for a cousin, Sir Lewis Stukeley, who is said to have died there in 1620. It was also the resort of pirates: one, William Salkeld, set himself up on Lundy in 1609 as 'King' and put cannons on the castle parade, and another, John Nutt, installed himself there in 1632 and took the title of 'Admiral'. In 1619 Lundy was given to Bevill Grenvile upon his marriage; he took great interest in his island, and never parted with it, despite pressing financial difficulties. The island was productive of butter and birds' eggs, and Sir Bevill had plans to profit by breeding horses there: 'I have lately made a quay and harbour there at my great cost, which the island ever wanted before' . . . 'I have so many reasons to be in love with it, as I shall never call it to sell or woo any man to buy it. . . .'[13] In 1643 Sir Bevill was killed, fighting for the royalist cause in the Civil War, and at some time the king appointed Thomas Bushell as governor of Lundy. Bushell claimed that he rebuilt the castle and fortified the island, and this was supported by Sir Bevill's son after the Restoration: '. . . touching my knowledge of his Services and Deportment in the time he commanded the Isle of Lundy . . . never person behaved himself more like a Gent . . . for he not only built the Castle from the ground at his own charge fit for any noble person to inhabit, but also . . . recovered several great guns whereby he defended the isle against all invasion, it being attempted to have been stormed with twenty Saile of Ships at one time.'[14]

The house that Bushell himself may have occupied is thought to be the one revealed by excavations at the south end of the parade in front of the castle, and which is seen in the engraving of 1775.[15] This 'Old House' had 'many of the features of a well-constructed and quite comfortable seventeenth-century dwelling. Windows and window-seats, bedding for floor joists, a fireplace, a cupboard, traces of mortar on the walls, and a domed clay oven. . . .'[16] The plan of the excavations and survey of 1988 shows evidence of three brick buildings (including a furnace) which appear to have been used in association with the Old House, but a definite date and purpose for these has not yet been established.

Bushell was a mining engineer with interests in silver mines, and he minted coins for the royal cause. Lundy was of obvious advantage to

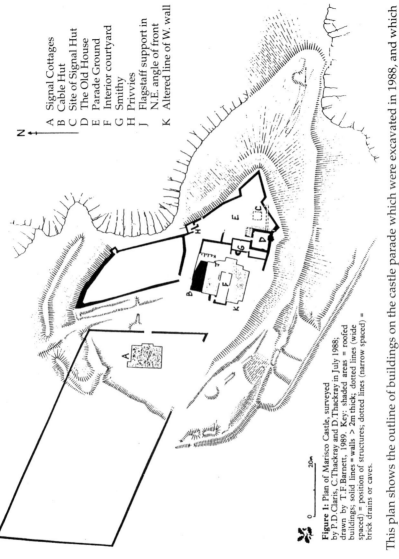

N

A   Signal Cottages
B   Cable Hut
C   Site of Signal Hut
D   The Old House
E   Parade Ground
F   Interior courtyard
G   Smithy
H   Privvies
J   Flagstaff support in
    N.E. angle of front
K   Altered line of W. wall

0 _____ 20m

Figure 1: Plan of Marisco Castle, surveyed by P.D.Claris, C.Thackray and D.Thackray in July 1988; drawn by T.F.Barnett, 1989. Key: shaded areas = roofed buildings; solid lines = walls > 2m thick; dotted lines (wide spaced) = position of structures; dotted lines (narrow spaced) = brick drains or caves.

This plan shows the outline of buildings on the castle parade which were excavated in 1988, and which are thought to date from the time of Bushell's occupation. The key has been superimposed. (*Lundy Field Society Annual Report* No 40, 1989.)

Thomas Bushell.

Thomas Bushell, born *c.* 1594 and died 1674. Governor of Lundy during the Civil War. (By permission of the British Library: BL 851.f.38.)

him by virtue of its impregnability, its position between his mines in Wales and North Devon, and – not least – the refuge it offered him from his creditors. He was loath to depart, and refused to surrender until he had the king's consent. He wrote, 'I have maintained Lundy at no other Contribution but my own, and how cheerfully I have exposed my friends and my own credit for your service, as well as exhausted them in the discovery of the Mines royall; besides the place in it self is useless, except in some advantages it may yield to me, if your sacred Majesty would be pleased to vouchsafe me leave to express my gratitude to my Lord Say by my quiet and free surrendering it, which I hope your goodness will not deny me, but if otherwise, your Majestie shall require my longer stay here; be confident Sir, I shall sacrifice both life and fortune, before the loyalty of Your obedient humble servant. . . .' The king's reply was, '. . . Now, since the place is unconsiderable in itself, and yet may be of great advantages unto you, in respect of your Mines, We do hereby give you leave to use your discreation in it, with this Caution, that you do take example from Our selves, and be not over-credulous of vain promises which hath made us great only in our sufferings, and will not discharge your debts.'[17] By this time the island belonged to Lord Say and Sele, who had bought it from the Parliamentarians after they sequestered the estates of Sir Bevill. The new owner was willing to sell it for £3,000 and Bushell tried to arrange an exchange of land, but this was not acceptable and so, as he had no money, the best he could do was to negotiate his terms of surrender. He had twenty men with him on the island at that time, and it was the very last royalist garrison to capitulate. By then, Bushell said, he had spent £5,570 on the castle and the garrison – huge sums at that time.

Lord Say and Sele's son, Richard Fiennes, went to Lundy to receive Bushell's surrender on February 24th 1647: '. . . according to . . . Mr

Bushell's promise, both me and my souldiers met him at the Kay of Crovelly, being the . . . nearest harbour to take shipping for Lundy, where we were forced to stay fifteen days for a winde, before we could arrive into the Road of Lundy; And his Lieutenant having notice that it was us by their Governour Mr Bushells shooting off a pistoll, gave us at our landing a salutation with all his Guns, and a volle of shot, as an entertainment of friendship, and free welcome, which made me confident of his former protest fidelity in surrendering the same, that both my selfe and my men marcht through his guard unto the Castle, commanding his own men to remain in another house, lest the ignorance of some men on both sides might beget a difference. . .; but so soone as they had understood the King's consent for surrender to the right Owner, and the Conditions made on their behalfe by their Governour . . . the morning tide following they took shipping for Ilford Combe . . . The Garisson being thus freely surrendered, with all things thereunto belonging, for Ammunition of Guns, and household-stuffe, according to his engagement upon the word of a Gentleman, but having demanded of his Lieutenant . . . what store of provision was left in the island, he replyed with a deep protestation, that for six monthes before Mr Bushell went over to treat with your Excellency . . . they nor their Governour had not eaten a bit of bread in six months, nor scarce drunk a barrell of bear in two yeares, alleaging the occasion was the Governour's known losses by land and sea. . .'[17] These island inhabitants were not the first or the last to sustain themselves on rabbits, wildfowl and fish. Bushell was an engaging character, who developed an attachment to Lundy, but his enthusiasms outran both his purse and his prudence. At the Restoration his plea for compensation was unrewarded, and when he died his debts were found to amount to £120,000. His surrender of the island marked the end of direct royal interest in Lundy, and of the period when the castle was a fortified stronghold, though it remained the principal building until the farmhouse was built in the late eighteenth century.

Whether or not Bushell had a mint on Lundy is open to dispute. He had a deputy governor on the island, and was minting coins in Bristol up until the Roundheads took it in 1645, when he retreated to Lundy. Certainly it would have provided a safe place for him to keep bullion. If he minted coins on Lundy, there is no record of his being granted licence to do so, although it could have been a matter of expediency when the royalist mints at Oxford, Aberystwyth and Bristol had all been lost. The furnace recently excavated on the castle parade can not be taken as evidence for a mint, as it is not considered to have been suitable for that purpose.[18] Bushell was never backward in advertising his works, yet he made no claim to have had a mint on Lundy. Though

The entrance to Benson's Cave. There is a brick-built room to the left of the entrance, which has not yet been dated. (Drawing: John Dyke.)

clearly he would not have made such a claim had the operation been a clandestine one.

The other open question of Bushell's tenure of Lundy is whether or not he excavated the cave below the castle, now known as Benson's Cave. He would certainly have had the knowledge and experience to order the work, from his involvement with the Mines Royal in South Wales. Against this must be considered two questions: why would he have wanted to do so, and why is the cave so large and lofty if the answer is that he required it for the safe keeping of bullion or munitions? Although the entrance is now small (5 ft wide and just over 4 ft high) excavation has shown that the headroom was once greater than that; the interior is roughly 6 ft wide, 12 ft high, and 63 ft long.[19] Again, it should be noted that Bushell, who was never slow to seek credit for his works, did not mention construction of the cave.

After Bushell, the next occupant of the castle lived there in quiet seclusion. Lord Say and Sele retired to Lundy after the execution of the king, it was said in remorse for his support of the Parliamentarians. His island '. . . had only a pretty strong house like a castle. . . ', and he spent his time in writing. The date of his departure is uncertain, but he was resident in 1653, the same year that Parliament ordered 'Four files of musketeers' to be sent there, possibly because of continued trouble from pirates in the Channel. By 1659 the person in charge of Lundy was a Sir John Ricketts, about whom nothing more is known.[20]

When Charles II was restored to the throne in 1660 Lundy was given back to the Grenvile family and Bevill's son, John, was created Earl of Bath. For many years Lundy was at different times both the resort of pirates and the victim of them. Smuggling was another possibility afforded by Lundy's particular configuration. One lessee, Richard Scores, used the island about 1721 to store smuggled goods, which were eventually seized by the customs officers, and he was forced to leave.[20] After that it seems that the island was probably uninhabited until 1748, when it was leased to Thomas Benson, a prosperous merchant in North Devon, and M.P. for Barnstaple. He was another remarkable character, whose designs on the island went beyond mere smuggling. He had contracted with the government to ship convicts overseas, the government's understanding being that they would be taken to Virginia. But Benson took them to Lundy, which he claimed 'was the same as sending them to America; they were transported from England, it mattered not where it was, so as they were out of the kingdom'.[21]

A visitor in 1752 wrote that, 'The island was at this time in no state of improvement; the houses miserably bad; one on each side of the platform; that on the right was inhabited by Mr Benson and his friends; the other by servants. The old Fort was occupied by the convicts, whom he had sent there some time before, and employed in making a wall across the island; they were locked up every night when they returned from their labour . . . The path to the house . . . was so narrow and steep, that it was scarcely possible for a horse to ascend it. The inhabitants, by the assistance of a rope, climbed up a rock, in which were steps cut to place their feet, up to a Cave or magazine, where Mr Benson lodged his goods. . .' Cannons were evidently in place, as 'There happened to come into the road, one evening, near twenty sail of vessels, which induced us to turn out early next morning to see them weigh their anchors, and sail. The colours were hoisted on the fort, and they all, as they passed Rat island returned the compliment, excepting one vessel, which provoked Mr Benson to fire at her himself, with ball, though we used every argument in our power to prevent him'.[22]

Despite the escape of some of the convicts, who took the island longboat and disappeared to Hartland, Benson evaded trouble until he over-reached himself in the design of an insurance fraud in the following year. He arranged for one of his ships to unload its cargo on Lundy before it was set on fire in the channel and sunk. The plot was discovered and Benson was ruined. He fled to Portugal in December 1753, and the captain of the ship, who had refused to turn King's evidence, was left to suffer capital punishment. Benson was described in the popular press as '. . . an enemy, not to one country only, but to the world, as the pest of society, and a disgrace to mankind.'[21]

The idea of an island castle with a secret tunnel is intriguing. It is certain that Benson used the cave to hide smuggled goods but he did not construct it, since the earliest of the inscriptions scratched on the inside walls dates from 1726. It is suggested that he might have enlarged it, and it was said that 'It was occasionally locked up'.[22] The date of its excavation can only be surmised, and it is remarkable that no account of the island before 1752 mentions it. It is possible that it was constructed when the castle was built as a place for safe storage, a refuge, or even a place to confine prisoners, since it would have been impossible to excavate beneath the castle itself for those purposes. Analysis of the mortars suggests a similarity between the cave and the Beacon Hill chapel, and as this is considered to date from the 12th or 13th century, the date of the cave could be the same as the date of the castle itself. But it is more probable that the mortars represent repairs or alterations made later than the original constructions, and Bushell might well have rebuilt this chapel in addition to his other works.[23] A capstan is shown in front of the cave in the 1776 engraving, and when the old steep narrow path up from the beach was the only access, with haulage of loads very difficult, it would have been a great advantage to be able to pull some cargoes up by ropes instead.

After the busy years of Benson's tenure only one family was left as caretakers, and Lundy was for many years in the hands of executors until it was bought by Admiral Sir John Borlase Warren in 1777. Two engravings show the castle as it was at this time, together with a clear ground plan. The accompanying description merely says '. . . there is a good beach, leading to a path made by art up the rock to the dwelling-house or castle. . . . The castle has large outworks, and was surrounded by a ditch, which may be traced in many parts.'[24] Sir John was another enthusiast who set about the improvement of his island, but he went off to war and sold it after only four years.

In 1787 a visitor gives this description: 'We walked in the evening to the Castle; (or rather its scite) the Castle is entirely demolished. It stood on the extremity of the south part of the island, facing Hartland Point,

The interior of Benson's Cave is surprisingly lofty. There are initials, dates and tally marks scratched on the walls, and remains of a cobbled floor. (Photo: Christopher Wright.)

on two acres of ground, and was surrounded by a stone wall with a ditch, excepting towards the sea, on the south, where the rock is almost perpendicular; the ditch appears very visible, and part of the walls, though most of them has been destroyed for the purpose of building offices for farming. The walls of the Citadel are very perfect, of a square form; it is converted into modern dwellings, the turrets which were chimneys still serve the same purpose, of which there are four – one at each angle. The south-west wall is nearly 51 feet, the north-west 38 and a half. In front of the house five guns are planted. The garrison was supplied with water from a spring which rises above the house built by

The castle from the north-east, 1775 (Grose, ibid). The Old House is seen far left.

The interior of the castle, with cottages, 1896. The girl in the photograph is Miss Sylvia Heaven. (Photo: Miss Eileen Heaven's collection.)

Sir John Warren; it was conveyed from thence in earthen pipes. . . . At the extremity of the rock, within the fortification, is a Cave, supposed to be cut out of the rock for a repository, store-room or magazine for the garrison: its form shews its great antiquity.'[22] From this it is clear that most of the castle (that is the whole complex including outworks) had been cleared and the stone used for other purposes, while the fort itself remained.

The castle was put to renewed use around this time, when the interior was converted to provide housing. The description quoted above suggests that it was Sir John Borlase Warren or Sir John Cleveland who carried out this conversion. Chanter says that Irish labourers brought in by Sir Vere Hunt destroyed '. . . all the remaining woodwork, and amongst other things, the old entrance gates and posts which had been placed there at the time when the castle was prepared for the refuge of Edward II'.[25] That the gates were put in place for Edward II cannot be relied on, but there were two of them: one to the north, giving access from the path up from the beach, and the other to the west, at the path leading into the island.

After Sir John Borlase Warren had either constructed or, possibly,

16

The interior of the castle and cottages today. (Photo: author.)

repaired the house which subsequently became the farmhouse (and then the Manor Farm Hotel), the centre of habitation again moved away from the castle to what is now termed 'the village'.

When Mr William Hudson Heaven bought Lundy in 1836 a new era of peaceful domestication began and, for the first time, the island came under the benign control of a resident owner. He made his home there after 1851, and as there was need for housing for his work people, the castle was brought back into use. The walls were repaired, and within them Mr Heaven constructed (or reconstructed) three cottages around a central courtyard. There were two tenements in each of the north and south cottages, and one tenement in the end cottage to the east. Probably at the same time the entrance in the west wall was extended to give protection from the wind, and for some reason a millstone was halved and incorporated into the steps at the entry. There are some privvies (earth closets) at the north-east edge of the platform, but it is not certain when they were put there. After the quarry company left Lundy other cottages became available, but one of the castle cottages was still occupied as late as 1891, and even after that they continued to be used for seasonal fishermen, occasional labourers, and stranded visitors.

Lloyd's Signal Hut from the west, ruins of Old House in the foreground.
(Photo: Miss Eileen Heaven's collection.)

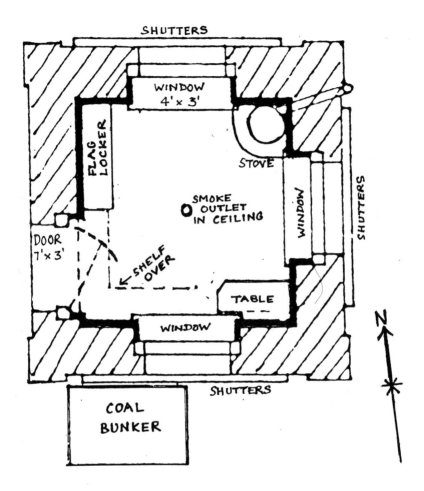

SHUTTERS

WINDOW 4' × 3'

FLAG LOCKER

STOVE

SMOKE OUTLET IN CEILING

WINDOW

SHUTTERS

DOOR 7' × 3'

SHELF OVER

TABLE

WINDOW

N

SHUTTERS

COAL BUNKER

INTERIOR DIMENSIONS 7 × 7 FT

Plan of Lloyd's Signal Hut 1905. (Public Record Office: Admiralty 116/957. Legend amended.)

The year 1884 heralded changes to come in the tenor of life on Lundy. Until then the island was still remote, but a combination of several factors caused it gradually to become more open to the outside world. Not long after the death of William Hudson Heaven (1883), the island was leased to tenants, so that only a small part of it was then the exclusive preserve of the Heaven family. There was an increase in the number of pleasure steamers coming to the island with excursionists, and a government post office was installed in 1887. Meanwhile, telegraphic communication with the mainland was installed, and this brought new life to the environs of the castle.

Until 1884 the castle had stood alone at the south-east corner of Lundy, but when the Rev. Mr Heaven made an agreement with Lloyd's for the establishment of a signal station, some new structures were put up nearby. Lloyd's built a look-out station with a fine view of the Channel to the south-east of the castle, close to where the remains of the Old House can now be seen, and this housed the signal flags and apparatus. A staff for Lloyd's flag was put up that was 68 ft high, and topped with a very large weathercock, and a signal mast was erected by the hut. Lastly, a pair of semi-detached cottages was built to the north-west of the castle to house the telegraph and Lloyd's signalmen. They kept a dawn-to-dusk watch on the movements of shipping up and down the channel, reports were sent back to Lloyd's, and messages could both be received for ships in the Roads and accepted from them for onward transmission. For the islanders, the arrival of the telegraph was a very welcome and significant event; up till then all news and messages arrived as and when boats came, and even urgent telegrams could be many days old when they were eventually delivered. Summoning help in emergency, either by boat or by beacons, had meant that the help could arrive too late. Unfortunately the submarine cable was prone to frequent breakdowns, and there were many occasions when the telegraph was 'sick', but signal flags and Morse apparatus were in use as well, and were the only resource when the cable finally broke in 1888.

In 1893 the G.P.O. took over the telegraph service, replaced the broken cable with a new one, and in the following year put up a new building to house it. Ancient buildings were not regarded with so much reverence at that time, and a lean-to was put against the north wall of the castle itself, the contractor being the lessee, Mr Ackland. This cable hut had a lobby and a main room with a fireplace, bunk beds, pigeon holes for messages, and the point of entry of the cable can still be seen on the west wall on the outside. The last of the additions made to the parade in 1893 was a semaphore signal apparatus. Thus, on a photo taken from the west soon after this, three projections can be seen above

Mr F. Allday, his wife and daughter, with another, outside Signal Cottages and post office, 1906. The notice above the door reads 'Postal Telegraph Office'. (Photo: Mrs C. Maddy.)

THE CASTLE ON THE ISLAND OF LUNDY

The Cable Hut, with the wooden shutters closed. The telegraph pole carried the wires for the telephone to the Villa (Millcombe), the Stores, the Bungalow (Brambles) and the Old Light, connected in 1893. (Photo: Society for the Protection of Ancient Buildings, 1928.)

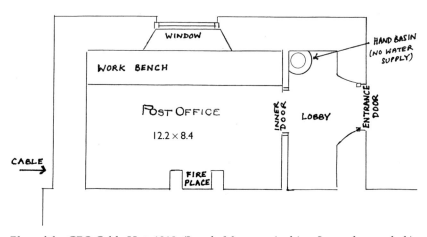

Plan of the GPO Cable Hut, 1918. (Lundy Museum Archive. Legend amended.)

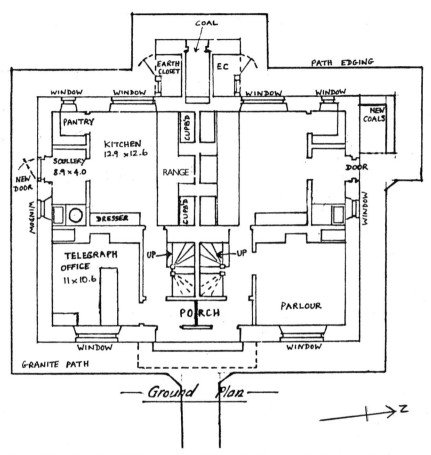

Plan of Lloyd's Signal Cottages 1905. The post office counter is shown in the south-east room. (Public Record Office: Admiralty 116/957. Legend amended.)

the roof of the castle – the flagpole carrying Lloyd's flag, the signal mast, and the semaphore mast.

Mr Frederick Allday came to Lundy as Lloyd's signalman in 1896, and when he took on the extra job of postmaster in 1898, the post office was moved from the Stores to Signal Cottages. The Allday family had both cottages, the telephone was in the back room, and there was a large counter in the south front room, which was the telegraph and post office. The mail day was on Thursdays (weather permitting) and the boat waited

The Coastguard Cottages built for the Admiralty in 1906. (Photo: H. Jukes, 1920. Lundy Field Society.)

The Coastguard Cottages and Watchroom, 1952. (Photo: A. & M. Langham.)

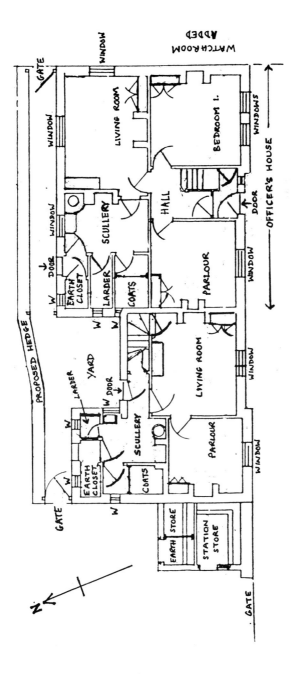

Plan of the Coastguard Cottages 1905. (Public Record Office: Admiralty 116/957. Legend amended.)

two hours, so that it was possible to send off immediate replies. In 1909 the post office was moved once again, this time to the cable hut, and the small postbox was attached to the telegraph pole. From the time of his first arrival on Lundy, Allday did not go ashore again until 1920, when he went to consult a doctor, and for the first time saw motor carriages on the roads.

The last of the buildings to be added to the castle environs was a pair of semi-detached cottages to the west of the castle, which were provided for their personnel when the Admiralty set up a watching station on Lundy in 1906. These were known as the Coastguard Cottages. Between 1920 and 1925 a watchroom was added at the eastern end that had in it a powerful telescope and a heating stove, but why a watchroom was sited where the view to the east was obstructed by the castle remains unexplained. In 1909 the Admiralty took over surveillance and signalling from Lloyd's, a new look-out and signal station was built at Tibbetts, and the hut on the castle parade fell into disuse. Mr Allday was retired from Lloyd's on pension, and as the Admiralty also had the use of Signal Cottages, he went to live at Quarter Wall cottages until he was able to lease the Cliff Bungalow (Hanmers) in 1920. He continued as postmaster until he left the island in 1927. The two Signal Cottages were in use for staff accommodation and holiday cottages until they were removed by the Landmark Trust in the course of the restoration of the whole castle site.

In 1927 the post office on Lundy was closed down, the following year the cable broke down, and the cable hut became known as 'The Keep'. After that it was only used occasionally for accommodation until 1960, when it was extended and converted for holiday letting, and re-christened Castle Cottage. It is still in use: 'it makes such a good place to spend a holiday, with a wonderful view, that we have not had the heart to demolish it'.[26]

For Mr Harman the castle seemed to embody the proud isolation of Lundy itself, and he invited the Society for the Protection of Ancient Buildings to survey it and make recommendations in 1928. Unfortunately he was not able to finance the work that was needed, but the report (given below) is of interest in evaluating the history of the construction.

When the Landmark Trust undertook their work on Lundy in 1969 the preservation of the castle was one of the earliest concerns, and repairs were carried out over several years until the careful restoration was completed. In consultation with the Department of the Environment, the three interior cottages have been reconstructed on the Victorian model, so that they serve to support and protect the structure. The dilapidated modern buildings on the surrounding land have been removed, and once again the castle stands in isolated and simple grandeur.

The visitors who may now spend their holidays in the castle cottages can enjoy their place in the newest stage of Lundy's oldest building, and 'the pleasures of escape and the pleasures of participation' that the island offers.[26]

The castle in 1993.

Notes

1 Paris, Matthew, *Chronica Majora*, Ed. H.R. Luard, London 1872–83
2 Liberate Rolls 1242–1243
3 Gardner, K., 'The Archaeology of Lundy', in Langham, A. & M., *Lundy*, 1980
4 Inq. 3 Edw I, No 54
5 *The History of the King's Works* Vol 2, HMSO 1963, 732
6 Close Rolls 1244
7 Patent Rolls 29 Henry III
8 Beamish, T., *Battle Royal*, London 1965
9 Patent Rolls 1264, 1265
10 Charter Rolls 1281
11 Calendar of Inquisitions 15 Edw II, No 49
12 *Devon Feet of Fines*, Vol 2, Devon & Cornwall Record Soc. 1939
13 Stucley, J., *Sir Bevill Grenvile & His Times*, Chichester 1983
14 Bushell, T., *Petitionary Remonstrance*, 1664
15 Dunmore, S., 'The Castle in the Isle of Lundy', *Devon Archaeological Society Proceedings* No 40, 1982. Readers can obtain copies of this work for a detailed account of the excavations
16 *National Trust Archaeological Survey* 1989, Vol I
17 Bushell, T., *A Brief Declaration of Severall passages in the Treaty concerning the Surrender of the Garrison of Lundy* 1647
18 Caroline Thackray, personal communication
19 Mills, M., *The Caves of Lundy*, Lundy Field Society Annual Report 19, 1968
20 Thomas, J., 'A History of Lundy from 1390 to 1775', *Transactions of the Devonshire Assn.* Vol 110, 1978
21 Thomas, S., *The Nightingale Scandal*, Bideford 1959
22 *North Devon Magazine* 1824. Stanley Smith uncovered some of the water pipes in the 1930s
23 Langham, A.F., *Preliminary investigations into building mortars used on Lundy*, Lundy Field Society, Annual Report No 20, 1969
24 Grose, F. *The Antiquities of England & Wales* Vol 4, 1776
25 Chanter, J. *Lundy Island*, London, 1887
26 *The Landmark Handbook*, 1993

Sources in addition to the above:

Gardner, K.S., *Archaeological Investigations, Lundy, 1964*, Lundy Field Society Annual Report 16, 1963–4

Gough, J.W,. *The Superlative Prodigal*, Bristol, 1932

The Heaven Family Diaries, Log and Letters 1871–1905, MSS

Illustrated Lundy News: No 9 1972, No 14 1974

Langham, A.F., *Thomas Benson's convict slaves on Lundy*, Lundy Field Society, Annual Report No 40, 1989

Langham A.F., *The Pirates of Lundy*, privately printed (undated)

Langham A. & M., *Lundy, Bristol Channel*, privately printed, 1960

Langham A. & M., *Lundy* 2nd Ed., David & Charles, Newton Abbot, 1984

Langham, M.S., *A Lundy Album*, privately printed, 1980

Langham, M.S., 'The Heaven Family of Lundy 1836–1916', *Transactions of the Devonshire Assn.* 118, 1986

The National Trust Archaeological Survey: Lundy, Devon Vols I & II, Caroline Thackray 1989

Steinman, G.S., 'Some Account of the Island of Lundy', *Collectanea Topographica et Genealogical*, Vol 4, 1837

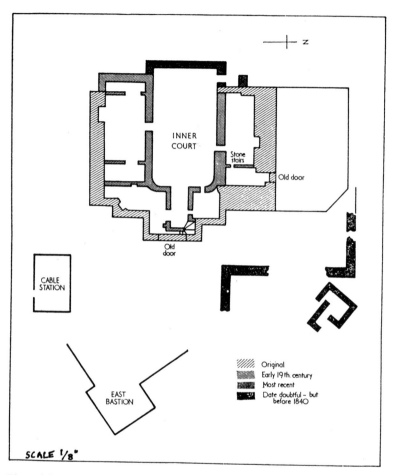

Plan of the castle shows how the west wall had been extended and suggests the building sequence. The cable station is inaccurate. (Charles Winmill, Society for the Protection of Ancient Buildings, 1928.)

Extract from *Report of Marisco Castle, Lundy, June 1928* Charles C. Winmill, Society for the Protection of Ancient Buildings.

'The original walling outside is built so as to incline inwards. The only part that I was able to plumb (on the sheltered north east angle) has a batter of 10 inches in 18 feet.' (Batter is the inward incline from the perpendicular).

'The plan of the castle and adjacent walling I have drawn to ⅛" scale. I have also prepared a site plan to approximately the same scale as the excellent . . . (1776) steel engraving . . . If this site plan is examined, we are able to judge as to the degree of accuracy shewn by the 1776 plan; the question then arises, to what extent can that plan be regarded as a correct statement of what then existed? Note the relative sizes of the East Bastion and the Castle, the Castle measured by me is practically the same as on the 1776 plan, whilst the bastion is very much larger than the one on the plan, and I think it will be evident that not much value can be attached to the old plan as to the position of the walls and enclosures said to exist in 1776 . . . the 18th century drawing . . . is of more value as a statement than the plan. It will be seen that the small corner towers are indicated in the view, but the embattlements, the embrasures of which are now partly walled up, are not indicated. An examination of the actual building shows that the towers, which are about five feet in diameter externally, have in recent years been used as chimney stacks, and are not corner bastions . . . had it not been for the old view might have been taken for modern work . . . embattlements and towers may have formed part of the original structure, but the present ones, in character, walling and especially the tabling below the towers at the extreme angles, give one the impression that those existing are not authentic work.'

In the photographs which accompany the report a large earthenware 19th century drain pipe is seen below the old east door. In the photograph of the castle in Loyd's book (1925) the small arc-shaped construction in the angle of the walls at the north-east corner holds a flagpole. This is not shown on Winmill's plan.

Keepers of Lundy and the King's Castle

(Owners shown in bold type)

1242	**Lundy forfeit to the Crown (Henry III)**
1242	William de Romare, Constable
1243	Richard de Especheleg, Constable
1244–1245	Richard de Clifford, Constable
1245–1250	Henry de Tracy, Keeper
1250–1251	Robert de Walerond, Keeper
1251–	William la Zouche, Keeper
1254–1281	**Edward, the king's son (Edward II in 1272)**
	William la Zouche, Keeper
–1264	Mauger de Sancto Albino, Keeper (King's party)
1264	Ralph de Wylenton, Keeper July–Sept. (Barons' party)
1264–1265	Humphrey de Bohun, Keeper (Barons' party)
1265	Adam de Gurdon, Keeper (King's party)
1265–1266	William de Valencia, Earl of Pembroke, Keeper (the king's half-brother)
1266–	Edmund, the king's brother, Keeper
	Lord Oliver de Dinan, title uncertain
1274	Geoffrey de Shauketon, Keeper
1275–	Lord Oliver de Dinan, lessee
1279	Richard De Insula (?)
1281–1284	**Sir William de Marisco, ownership restored**
1284–1289	**Sir John de Marisco, his son**
1289	**Herbert de Marisco, his son**
1290	Rotheric de Weylite, Custodian appointed by the king during the minority of Herbert
	Olivia de Marisco, widow of Sir John, claimant
1300–1321	**Olivia de Marisco**
1321–1326	**Herbert de Marisco (died 1326)**
–1322	**Sir John de Wyllenton, lands forfeit to the Crown**
1322–1326	**Hugh, Lord Despencer the Younger, and his wife**
	By grant of Edward II. Hugh executed 1326
1326	**Lundy forfeit to the Crown; Prince Edward Guardian of the Realm**
1326	William de Kerdestan, Keeper
1326–1327	Otto de Bodrigan, Keeper
1327	Philip, Lord de Columbers & William de Botereux?
1327	**Estates restored to Sir John de Wyllenton**
1327–1332	**Sir Ralph de Wyllenton held Lundy of his father**
1332	**William de Montacute, First Earl of Salisbury, by purchase**

Inhabitants of the Castle Cottages
1851–1891

1851

2 inhabited houses	William Burman	Head	42	Ag. labourer
	Esther Burman	Wife	41	Dressmaker
	Eliz. Burman	Daughter	13	Scholar
	Mary Ann Burman	Daughter	8	Scholar
	Sarah Burman	Daughter	5	Scholar
	Selena Burman	Daughter	2	
	Samuel Sexon	Servant	14	Servant/Ag. labourer

1 inhabited house	Robert Vanstone	Head	43	Cooper
	Ann Vanstone	Wife	45	Laundress
	Sarah Vanstone	Daughter	16	Servant
	Mary Ann Vanstone	Daughter	11	Scholar
	John Vanstone	Son	8	Scholar

1861 No details available

1871

Castle No 1	Thos Withycombe	50	Labourer	Head
	Ann Withycombe	57	Housewife	
	Henry Board	39	Ag. labourer	Unm. Lodger

Susanna Spearman	67	Widow	Head
Eliz. Spearman	24	Dressmaker	Daughter
John Lugg	25	Whitesmith	Marr. Boarder

Castle No 2	Joseph Dark	35	Carpenter	Head
	Mary Dark	47	Housewife	
	Margaret Dark	9	Daughter	
	Dora Dark	7	Daughter	
	Ellen Dark	5	Daughter	
	Florence Dark	11mo.	Daughter	
	William Pickard	54	Master mariner	Marr. Lodger

Castle No 3 Uninhabited

1881
Cottages 1 & 2 Uninhabited

Cottage No 3	Christopher Ward	Head	Marr.	45	Gardener
	Louisa Ward	Wife	Marr.	44	
	Mary Ward	Daughter	Unm.	16	
	Annie Louisa Ward	Daughter	Unm.	5	Scholar
	Nicholas Jeffery	Lodger	Marr.	64	Mason

1891

1	Inhabited cottage	George Parsons	Head	Single	23	Under gardener
2	Uninhabited cottages					

NB. The castle was within the area reserved for the Heaven family, and the inhabitants of the castle cottages were their employees.

From: Census Returns, Public Record Office
HO 107/1985. RG: 9/1505, 10/2207, 11/2262